ReWired

A Story of Recovery from Spinal Cord Tumor Surgery

Dawn Standera

DEDICATION

To my Sherpas,
for being with me on every step of the journey.

CONTENTS

The appendix includes a video link and a transcript of Dawn Standera's presentation at the 2015 Spinal Tumor Patient Education Conference at the MD Anderson Cancer Center. The talk not only chronicles Dawn's five-year journey of coping with the tumor and its symptoms, it also highlights her insights into the unique and difficult decision faced by spinal cord tumor patients about whether or not to have tumor-removal surgery.

INTRODUCTION

The first thing I remember after surgery is being able to move my hands and feet and breathe on my own. I remember smiling. I was not paralyzed. My neurosurgeon later told me that I said, "I'm a rock star." I probably did. It sounds like something I would say.

For the record, I am not a rock star. I am a spinal cord tumor (SCT) survivor. I survived living with it, and I survived the surgery that removed it.

In 2011 I was diagnosed with an intramedullary tumor. "Intramedullary" means that it had originated in the spinal cord. We wanted to know, of course, if it was malignant. Normally with tumors, a bit of it is removed and a biopsy is done to determine if you have cancer or not. The problem with tumors inside the spinal cord is that you don't always get a biopsy, which means you don't find out if it's cancer until after the tumor is removed. Cutting into the spinal cord—for reasons you are about to read— is a dangerous procedure, so a biopsy wasn't an option in my case.

The tumor's location was of critical importance. It was not on the bony spinal column, nor was it on the outside of the spinal cord; it was on the *inside* the spinal cord itself. The tumor was surrounded by nerves and healthy cord tissue—basically everything that made my body "work." The only way to get rid of the tumor was to cut through the healthy part of my spinal cord. In other words, undergoing surgery meant causing a spinal cord injury.

It gets worse. A tumor can appear anywhere in the spinal cord, but the higher up in the spinal cord it is, the more damage it can cause the body. Mine was growing at the very tip-top of the cord, at cervical levels 1 and 2 (C1-C2). If damage happens to you at C1-C2, you risk becoming a quadriplegic. Think of movie star Christopher Reeve *(Superman)*—in 1995 he was thrown from a horse and shattered his C1-C2, resulting in paralysis from the neck down.

So you can see why I smiled as I moved my hands and feet after surgery and declared myself a rock star when I realized the worst had not happened.

That was December 8, 2015.

After being diagnosed, I lived with the tumor for four years and ten months before I made the decision to risk the surgery that would remove it. This book is not about that part of my life. If you want to know what it's like to live with an SCT, or what it's like to face the agonizing decision of whether or not to have surgery, you can watch the presentation that I gave at the 2015 Spinal Tumor Patient Education Conference at the MD Anderson Cancer Center in Houston, Texas. (A link to the video and a transcript of the presentation are included in the

2

Appendix of this book.) Adult SCTs are very rare, and those of us who choose to watch-and-wait for surgery are hungry for information and for the hope of connecting with someone else in the same circumstance. That is why I made the presentation at MD Anderson.

During the time leading up to surgery, I wanted to read about other people's experiences, but as far as I could tell there were no books or pamphlets written by adult survivors of SCT surgery. Someone should write about it, that much I knew. I thought long and hard about whether that someone should be me, or if I should just put the whole affair in my rearview mirror. Then I realized I could do both: I could move forward and put the experience behind me by telling my story.

PREPARING FOR SURGERY

Adults with SCTs are exceedingly rare. Rarer still are those who have a tumor as high in the cord as mine was. I was desperate to get a sense of what life after surgery might be like. I was told things would be "different," but what did that mean? What would it feel like? Could I tolerate it? Would things improve and, if so, how fast and how far?

I was diagnosed at age 45, and it wasn't until four years later I connected with Jennifer, a woman who had survived the surgical removal of a C2-C4 tumor. My medical team had put me in contact with her several months before surgery. As we spoke on the phone, I hung on her every word, asking all the questions that I had bottled up inside for years. I thanked her for her time, got off the phone and had a good cry. After years of living with the SCT, after having no one to talk to who had lived through the surgery, I was overcome with emotions. My husband, Tony, wanted to hear all about it. My family and friends wanted to hear all about it. We had waited for some connection, some information, and when we got it we felt better. Only a survivor could provide the kind of personal, experiential information that Jennifer offered. I had an excellent medical team, but I never heard a word about these kinds of things from them because they really couldn't tell me—they never had the experience. The experience belongs to the patient.

The week before surgery, I received a phone call from another surgery survivor, a woman named Carol (a friend of mine in Boston put her in touch with me). Twelve years earlier, Carol had undergone the same surgery that I was now facing. I clearly remember Carol telling me this: *Remember that the way you feel when you wake up from surgery is not the way you will feel forever.* That statement became my mantra.

Going into surgery, I had two rules for myself:

1) No labels. I knew things were going to get weird. What was about to happen to me was not something I could think my way through, so I decided that I would not label any experience as *good* or *bad.* If I let my mind race ahead of my body, I would jump to conclusions—jump to labeling—and that would only confine me in *a this is good* vs. *this is bad* way of thinking. I vowed to not push toward predetermined endpoints in my mind.

2) Stay curious, grateful, composed and graceful, and never lose a sense of humor.

In retrospect, these turned out to be valuable rules, as they helped guide me through the most bizarre sensory experiences—and the most challenging physical experiences—of my life.

WAKING UP FROM SURGERY
DAY ONE

When I woke up from surgery, my body felt numb and I could not determine the outline of my body from my collarbone to my toes. It felt like my nerves were reaching beyond the boundary of my skin. The only parts of my body that felt normal were my shoulders and above. The strange thing about the numbness is that I could *feel* things—my body sensed touch—but it was not in the same way I had felt things before. I could feel the medical staff poke me with sharp vs. dull objects and could tell the difference between them, but it almost felt like it was happening to someone else's body. Another way to describe it is that it felt like there was an energetic force field around my body and when people touched me it felt like they were touching the edges of the force field and not actually touching my body.

My whole body felt like it was floating off the bed, and it felt like my feet were on the ceiling and my head was on the bed—like I was standing on my head while lying in bed. It took all my concentration and energy to make peace with the sensory experience I was having.

During those first couple of days I clung to my mantra: *I am not going to feel like this forever.*

At the same time I was full of gratitude that the surgery was a success and that it looked like the tumor was completely removed. I was proud of my neurosurgeon, proud of myself for taking the risk and proud of my body for making it through the surgery successfully. I remember waking up from surgery, seeing my family standing next to my bed and I said, "I did it". I guess that summed it up.

The experience of not being embodied was unlike anything I could have imagined. It felt like my nerves were trying to find a way home to my body; a body I could not feel. The image I had in my mind was of a million strings made of light reaching out from every part of my body, searching throughout the universe, as if they were seeking to make sense and order of this new circumstance. It's hard to describe, but I felt boundless. It made me wonder if that is how we really are if we didn't have bodies.

During the lead-up to surgery, I was told that my sensory system would be impaired in some way after surgery. This happens because the surgical cut is made into the *back* side of the spinal cord (where the sensory nerves live) instead of into the front of the cord (where the motor nerves live). Simply put, sensory nerves deliver information to the brain about touch, sounds, etc.; motor nerves allow the brain to control such things as muscles. I tried and tried to prepare myself mentally, tried and tried to imagine what I might feel like post-op, but trust me, there is no frame of reference for the experience.

I was instructed to lie flat for 24–48 hours after surgery, to prevent the leakage of cerebral spinal fluid—something which would cause a spinal headache to develop. I was unable to turn my head due to neck pain and stiffness from the incision. I was allowed to "log roll" (keep my body aligned as a unit while I rolled to one side or the other on a flat bed), but I wasn't able to do it by myself because I couldn't feel my body; I simply couldn't make sense of how to get my arms and legs to do something that complicated. I think it was about 36 hours before I was physically able to roll over in bed by myself.

During the first 48 hours, I was miserable with unrelenting nausea and frequent vomiting. Turns out it is possible, but highly unpleasant and dangerous, to vomit while lying flat on your back. (According to my husband, I do a great *Exorcist* scene re-enactment.) The staff tried all kinds of medications to treat the nausea, but none of them worked. At this point I will tell you that I'm a registered nurse, which means I have a keen understanding of the dangers of vomiting on your back and what to do about it. Unfortunately, the nurse I had that night did not take my concerns seriously. Let me say right now—with the utmost emphasis—that the care I received in the hospital was *excellent*. Believe me, I am a tough critic. That being said, I did have one bad experience and it happened on the first night. I am somewhat reluctant to detail the experience because I don't want to "bad mouth" the staff *and* because I don't like reliving the memory of that first night. But it happened, so here we go.

The first problem was that I was unable to use the nurse call light at my bedside. The reasons were: (1) the buttons on the call light were flat and I simply couldn't feel them, (2) I didn't have the range of motion in my neck to lift my head to look at the buttons, and, (3) I didn't have enough coordination in my hands to lift the call light up to my eyes to see the buttons. When I brought this to the nurse's attention, she showed me how to push the buttons, but my fingers just wouldn't do it. I asked for another type of call light, but she said they didn't have one. I knew that couldn't be the case. As an RN, I have given "easy-to-use" call lights to patients who couldn't use the standard ones. (For whatever reason, I was able to get an easy-to-use one the next day.)

The second problem was that I was lying flat on my back and I knew I was going to vomit. Without a call light there was no way the staff could get to me in time to suction my airway. To solve this problem, I asked the staff to leave the suction unit turned on and to give me the suction catheter, so I could suction my own airway as needed. Then I asked the staff to call my family so that someone could stay with me during that first night. My husband and Mom showed up. My husband eventually couldn't keep his eyes open so my mom stayed with me.

My mom saved my life that night. She was my call light. I vomited several times. I would suction the vomit from my mouth so I didn't choke, then my mom would help me turn to my side and get the nursing staff to help her clean up the mess. God bless my dear mom. By the end of that night she had been awake over 24 hours and kept her daughter safe.

Not everyone will go through what we went through that first night. I happen to be someone who gets nauseated after surgery and vomits; not everyone does.

At first I wasn't going to write about this, but then decided it could be valuable to any medical staff who may want to change their practices to ensure an SCT patient can use their call light.

It could also be valuable to patients and families who may want to consider scheduling round-the-clock caregivers for those first few days. It's a good idea to choose someone who is comfortable with medical environments. Find someone who knows basic CPR and who knows how to roll you into recovery position so you can vomit while lying on your side, instead of your back.

DAY TWO

I spent most of the day trying not to vomit, and sleeping when I could. I was frequently roused by the staff who would come in to check my neurological status. They poked me with sharp things and dull things and asked if I could tell the difference (yes, I could). They moved my toes up and down and asked if I could tell which direction they were pointing (I could tell on my left foot, but had no idea on my right foot). They checked to see if the strength in my hands and feet was strong and equal (my right side was weaker). As it turned out, the tumor was attached to the right, interior wall of my spinal cord; its removal caused more damage to that side of the cord, resulting in more impairments to the right side of my body.

The medical staff did frequent assessments of my motor functions throughout my hospital stay. They wanted to know if I had weakness, if I had urinary continence, how was my balance, could I walk, how was my proprioception. If you've had a SCT, you'll know about proprioception testing (whether or not you call it by that name); it's when you're told to close your eyes, and, while a neurologist moves a toe up and down, you're asked if you

11

can tell if it's pointing up or down. Proprioceptors are found all over our body; their job is to help our brain perceive movement and recognize spatial orientation. Basically, proprioceptors tell our brain where our body exists in space. If a surgical cut is made into the spinal cord from the back side—the side where our sensory nerves live— our proprioception is compromised. Our amazing bodies can compensate somewhat, but that sense of knowing where we are in space is forever altered. It's a bitch.

Although my medical team was very attentive to my motor skills, they didn't seem much interested in hearing about how I *felt*. That I seemed disembodied. That I couldn't sense the outline of myself. That when I was lying in bed, it felt like I was floating and spinning in outer space. I don't mean to say that they were uncaring— nothing could be further from the truth—but their lack of fascination with my bizarre sensory experience surprised me. It soon became clear, however, that an altered sensory experience was to be expected, and it helped when I realized that's how they were viewing it.

I was scheduled to have an MRI on day two, but I was still so nauseated that I vomited whenever I tried to move. I was fairly certain I would vomit in the MRI, so I told them to delay the scan until my nausea was gone. Later that day, my nurse practitioner had a thought: it might help to try a medication that relaxed my diaphragm (cervical nerves innervate the diaphragm, and it was obvious that my cervical nerves were not happy after the surgery). That did the trick. Once the nausea and vomiting were over, I slept for most of day two.

My friend Peg (who is an experienced, excellent nurse with good common sense) flew in from Minnesota, and that night she stayed by my side. She did this for five nights. We arranged it so that my family would be with me during the day, and Peg would stay overnight in my room. Her time at my side gave my family the chance to get several nights of good sleep. It was such a relief having her there, not to mention a convenience, as I did not have to wait for hospital staff to assist me. If someone with whom you are comfortable offers to help, my advice is to take the offer. As the days passed and I was permitted to do more things, it was Peg who helped me to the bathroom, helped me bathe, helped me dress. She brainstormed new ways that I might try to do things that would keep me safe and more comfortable. She was a second set of ears to hear medical information. As we lay in our beds at night, she would listen as I verbally processed my experiences of the day. We did our fair share of laughing which we all know is the best medicine.

DAY THREE

My incision was about seven inches long. During surgery they did a laminectomy (a surgical procedure that removes a portion of the vertebral bone called the lamina) at C1, C2 and the very upper edge of C3. As I understand it, sometimes the parts of the bone they remove are put back in place with hardware and sometimes they aren't. In my case there was no hardware. They used a muscle flap closure instead.

Here is the description from the surgical report:

> Bilateral paraspinous muscles were mobilized and advanced. Lateral relaxing incisions were made to facilitate immobilization. The muscles were then approximated at the midline using a series #2 buried figure-of-eight suture Vicryls. It was then further imbricated into the defect using wider 2-0 Vicryls. The trapezius muscle was then closed at the midline to provide an additional layer of coverage using 2-0 Vicryls.

I did not experience a lot of pain at the incision site but it was very stiff and I had limited range if motion in my neck. The way I think about it and the way it feels to me is that the trazepezius and paraspinous muscles were "rearranged".

The nausea and vomiting had subsided. I was ready for the MRI and managed to get through it without puking. The result of the scan was just what we wanted to hear— the tumor was gone. Now we had to wait for the pathology report.

I knew that it was now time to get to work, and I hit the ground running (figuratively speaking). We live in a culture that rewards and praises overcoming adversity, and I was rewarded with lots of praise about my attitude. I was driven to get better. I was determined to be the star patient, the one who had the best outcome, who worked the hardest, who was admired by everyone. I think that ended up being mostly true, but I paid a price for it. I learned a hard lesson about my overzealous work ethic. I did not yet understand when to push and when to soften. In my defense, I did not realize the extent to which my body was sending me messages in a language I did not yet understand.

My first task on day three was to sit up in bed and keep my balance. The problem was that I did not *feel* like I was sitting on a bed. It felt like I was sitting on a giant ball. In fact, ever since the surgery I have had the constant sensation that I'm sitting on a ball. Right after surgery it felt like a huge exercise ball, but now it's smaller—some days a basketball, some days a softball, and on a good day, it's a golf ball. But always a ball.

Throughout day three I continued to practice sitting up in bed. It took intention and energy to stay upright. I was able to do it, but it tired me out in a way I didn't know existed. If I closed my eyes it felt like I was rolling around the top half of the ball and could easily tip over. My arms and legs did what they were told—sort of. Despite the challenges, I recall being euphoric and overwhelmed with gratitude that things were looking like they were going to be okay, and I knew that I would do the work needed to get better.

The most amazing outcome of the surgery was that the crushing headache I had endured 24/7 for three years was gone. *Gone.* My headache was the primary symptom that had pushed me over the surgery decision hurdle. I was told that the operation may or may not relieve the headache; it was a roll of the dice. So much of the SCT experience seems to be a roll of the dice. Up until that point, I had tried every intervention available to relieve the constant pain in back of my head, and nothing had worked. My intuition told me the tumor was to blame, and now it seemed my intuition was right.

Those first no-headache days had me giddy. The incision pain from the surgery was nothing compared to the absence of the headache pain. Even though it seemed the surgery might have messed up my right hand, that paled in comparison to not having the headache. I remained headache-free for three months, and then it started to show up again at some point during each day, but in a less painful form. Before surgery, the headache pain was non-treatable; after surgery, two ibuprofen usually take care of it. That being said, because I try to remain free of labels (my first rule) and remain curious (my second rule) I still have hope that the headache will once again disappear. I trust my intuition about my body. It has not failed me yet.

DAY FOUR

Now that I was able to sit up by myself, it was time to practice standing and walking. I did this with the help of my physical therapy (PT) team, a walker, and a gait belt that was cinched around me for safety. I could not feel my feet in contact with the floor. In fact, it felt like my feet were hovering about two feet above the floor. I stomped my feet, relying on my ears to tell me that my feet were in contact with the ground. My butt felt like it was way up in the air over my head, like a string pulled it up behind me. When I moved, it felt like my butt and legs were hovering over my head. I kept getting this image of the Macy's Thanksgiving Day Parade balloons, and the way they float down the street. It was very distracting. I relied on my eyes to tell me that my butt was under my abdomen, verifying that I was, in fact, standing upright and not floating. But I could *walk*. I could tell it was going to be a long process until it felt or looked normal, but the worst had *not* happened, I was *not* paralyzed. I felt overwhelmed with gratitude.

The next step was to find out if I was going to be continent. When the urinary catheter was removed, would I be able to sense the natural urge to urinate, and, if so, would I be able to control it? In other words, was I going to need diapers? I told the nurse that I could feel the catheter in me, which I took to mean I would likely be able to sense the need to urinate. The catheter came out and, happily, everything began working as it should. I was so grateful to have full control of my bladder and bowels, as this surgery is known to carry a significant risk of causing long-term incontinence.

Even though I am continent, things are still different in regard to going to the bathroom. To this day, the only way I can tell I'm done peeing is when I *hear* that I'm done. I wasn't aware of this until months later when I used the restroom in an airplane. It was noisy in there, and I suddenly realized that I couldn't tell if I was done peeing or not, because all this time I had been depending on my hearing to tell me. Now, whenever I'm in a noisy restroom, I just sit a really long time until it seems like I surely must be done.

For a while, right after surgery, everything my skin touched (including other skin) felt like sandpaper. I recall lying in bed feeling the skin of my legs touching each other, and when I pulled them apart it felt like Velcro tearing. It was so annoying that I began putting a cotton sheet between parts of my skin that touched any other skin. It was impossible to feel the difference between my skin and my clothes because it all felt the same—skin, clothes, bed, silverware—everything. I couldn't tell whether I had clothes on or not. To know for sure, I had to look, and that was a problem because I could barely turn my neck. So I used my other senses. I would pinch and pull on places where my clothes ought to be and listen for a snap. Or, I would try to sense a temperature change as the fabric moved. If all else failed, I would just ask someone if my butt was covered. More than once I'd sit down to urinate, and, when I went to use the toilet paper, I could tell something was weird. "Oh great," I would say, "I peed through my undies." I was not able to feel that I had forgotten to pull them down because the fabric and my skin felt exactly the same.

The whole tactile dysfunction issue did (and still does) drive me nuts. In the early weeks after surgery—in an attempt to retrain my brain—I would lie in bed, observe my fingers touch something, and then tell myself over and over what it was. For example, I would touch the sheets of the bed and repeat, "This is cotton. This is soft. This is fabric." It felt like my brain was a giant Rolodex and on every index card was an adjective describing what something might feel like. As I touched the sheets, my brain would run through the Rolodex cards trying to match a description to the sheets. My brain would say "peanut butter" and I would say, "No, not peanut butter; this is fabric," then my brain would say "water" and I would say, "No, not water; this is fabric." This would go on for a long time. For some strange reason, my brain wanted to tell me that a lot of things felt like peanut butter or glue or water or jelly or mud. I just kept repeating the process over and over and over with everything I touched. It was both tiring and fascinating.

Eventually, my brain relearned how to identify the way things should feel. When it was tired, however, it went back to its default of telling me that everything felt like sandpaper. A few months after surgery the sandpaper default changed to everything feeling like Naugahyde. Weird, but true. Although it's gotten better, it's not gone. To this day, when my brain starts defaulting to Naugahyde, I know my body is telling me I'm overtired. It's a part of the new language my body speaks. If I try to push through it, things get worse, so I just take a nap. Things usually get better once I'm rested.

In order to resolve tactile issues, Occupational Therapy (OT) worked with me on sensory retraining. They had me touch and retouch objects with diverse surfaces. I touched smooth things, rough things, prickly things, feathery things, and so on. The OT team worked with me on stereognosis, which is the ability to perceive solid objects by touch. For about three months I was unable to identify what was in my right hand if I did not see it. If my eyes were closed and an object was placed in my right hand, I could only tell it was there if it was colder or warmer than my hand, or if it was heavy. If the object was close to my body temperature, or was small and lightweight, I could not tell if my hand was empty or not.

The issue with my right hand resulted in some practical problems at home. For example, it was a challenge for me to wash dishes. When my hands were under the soapy water, I could neither see nor reliably feel what I was handling (especially silverware). After giving myself a few cuts on my fingers, we made it a rule never to put sharp knives in the dishwater. Thankfully, I never lost the capacity to feel hot and cold in that hand, which comes in handy in order to avoid frostbite or burns.

Another OT exercise was to have me find objects buried in a box of beans or rice using only my right hand, not my eyes. We started with large objects like balls and staplers, and eventually made it to beads and paper clips. (I hated trying to find paper clips—I doubt I could find them now.) These days I rarely think about not being able to feel what I have in my right hand. When I'm tired, however, my right hand begins to lose its ability to sense things.

At this point my left hand was still numb, but its motor function worked perfectly. Before surgery I had very little feeling in my left hand, though I did have a constant burning pain, and pins-and-needles sensations. After the

20

first couple of months the numbness went away completely, as did the burning, and the pins-and-needles feeling. Simply put, the surgery made my left hand feel and function better.

I did have to relearn how to feed myself. It was not a chewing or swallowing problem, it was a proprioception problem. After surgery I had deficits in my fine motor skills and a lack of proprioception in the right side of my body. My right hand was affected the most, and I was (of course) right-handed. Holding on to silverware (which I could not feel) and aiming to get a spoonful of food into my mouth was very challenging. I couldn't tell where my arm was in space. I would watch my arm doing aimless things and wonder why it wasn't following my brain's instruction to bring food to my mouth. I couldn't control it; the messages were just not getting through. As often as the food would make it to my mouth was about as often as it would make it to my ear, my chin, or my eye. Suffice it to say it was a long time before they allowed me to handle a fork.

As my work with the OT team advanced, so did the level of challenge to my proprioception, and to the motor skills of my right hand. My recollection of this time is that every task I had to relearn took all the courage, stamina and creativity I had to give. One of the most difficult tasks was learning to dress myself again—buttons and zippers became my mortal enemies. Typing on a keyboard was a seriously exhausting exercise. I had trouble holding a pen, and, once I was able to hold it, I had trouble getting the tip to the paper. In the beginning my handwriting was illegible. Over time it improved, but it took six months before I could recognize it as my own.

I needed someone nearby for safety whenever I showered. For ten weeks I had to use a shower chair, holding the spray head with one hand and the shower bar with the other, keeping my eyes closed as briefly as possible (when I closed my eyes I would lose my balance). Now I can shower without thinking much about it, though I do notice I touch the shower wall whenever I close my eyes under the spray. I'm not sure if I really need to do this—maybe it just a precaution, maybe just a learned habit.

DAY SIX

The pathology results came in, and my tumor was determined to be a Grade II conventional ependymoma. The tumor was out, and I was not going to need any follow-up radiation. It was what we expected, but a relief to finally hear it from the doctors.

My brother and his wife went home to Georgia. My parents went home to Florida. My friend (and personal nurse) Peg went home to Minnesota. Now it was just my husband and me, and as I began to face the thought of our going home, I learned an important lesson about myself.

It was day six after surgery when I realized that the staff thought I was doing better than I actually was. I had the feeling that they were going to send me home, and I knew I wasn't ready. Although I was making progress, I was still not able to shower, dress, walk, or negotiate stairs without assistance. If I couldn't sit in a chair for more than one hour, how was I supposed to handle the eight hours of effort it would take to fly home from Houston to Minnesota? I *knew* that I needed to stay right where I was for a course of inpatient rehab, but, at the same time, I knew plans were in motion for my discharge, and outpatient therapy back home. How could their perception of my ability to go home at this point be so different from mine?

After careful consideration, I came to realize that my *composure* was being misinterpreted as *competence*. It's like the old saying that the squeaky wheel gets the grease. In the medical world, the squeaky patient gets the rehab. I had approached my surgery with these themes: be curious, grateful, composed and graceful, and don't lose a sense of humor. I was determined to become as independent as possible as soon as possible. Were these very things now working against me? What was I to do? Panic? Cry? Not my style. So I decided to try plain old honesty.

I resolved to tell every physician and therapist that I met with that day about my concerns. I started with the neurosurgery fellow on morning rounds. The conversation went like this, "Doctor, I want to be clear with you about some concerns I have regarding my discharge planning. I know I've been doing exceptionally well in my recovery and in my attitude, and am grateful for this. However, I am concerned that staff is confusing my composure with my ability to be safe at home." I didn't get much of a response from him, but then, I never could read that guy. Neurosurgery fellows seem a strange bunch.

I persisted in telling my story to each staff member I interacted with that morning. I finally made a breakthrough with the physical therapist. He and I started on our morning walk and made it to the elevator (about a 100-foot walk) where I sat down to rest. That is where I told him my concerns. And that is where he confessed to me that, yes, he probably *was* confusing my composure with competence. He immediately did a new assessment on my ability to climb stairs, ambulate without rest, keep my balance without assist, etc. When he looked at me *subjectively*, I appeared to be far enough along to safely go home; when he evaluated me *objectively*, however, he saw I was not even close to being discharged safely. He said he learned an important lesson that day. I did too.

After the new assessment, we walked back to my room to find the medical staff going over discharge instructions with my very pale-looking husband. My PT immediately shared his concerns, and the decision was made to have me stay and do two weeks of inpatient rehab. What a relief.

For all of us who carry ourselves with composure—be aware of how this may be perceived, especially by medical personnel. We must be fully honest about our condition, first with ourselves, and then with others. We must speak with confidence and clarity so that our needs are well communicated and understood.

DAY EIGHT

Being in the hospital is like living in another culture. New language, new rules, and the King and Queen of Hospital Land are the insurance companies. Fortunately, it's not as foreign to me as it might be to others since I've worked in hospitals as an RN.

For the first three days after surgery I was a patient in the Neuro Intensive Care Unit (ICU). After that, I was placed in Neuro Step-Down status, but I stayed in the same room because there were no open beds in the Neuro Step-Down Unit. I was glad, as I had a really nice room and excellent care. Not being an ICU patient meant I no longer needed to be hooked up to the continual monitoring of blood pressure, arterial line, heart monitor, etc., and I was happy to be free from the tubes and lines and bells and whistles.

Physical therapy visited daily, and although we were working hard, I wanted more time with them. I wanted to get the inpatient rehab show on the road, but since I was not the Queen of this Land, the show was not going to go anywhere until (a) the hospital submitted the request, and (b) my insurance company agreed to it.

While waiting for word on inpatient rehab, Tony was there to help me walk as often as my body allowed. I couldn't walk very far, but I knew that getting out of bed frequently and taking short walks was better than getting out of bed for one long walk each day. At this point I was using a walker for ambulation, with stand-by assistance. I also did my OT exercises several times each day.

The hospital's request for inpatient rehab was made, and as we waited for insurance approval I started working with OT and PT personnel. They recommended I have inpatient therapy for three hours each day for at least two weeks. I was progressing well, but had a long way to go. My body was slowly thawing out and I was beginning to feel the presence of my left arm. I could dress and feed myself. We were still working on proprioception, motor skills, and strength building for whole right side of my body. Everyone, including me, was optimistic. The headache was gone. Life was exhausting. Every task took all the stamina and creativity I could muster. Still, I felt so grateful.

DAY ELEVEN

We received official word that the insurance company approved my inpatient rehab. My status was changed from Neuro Step-Down to Rehab. It was Friday, and not much structured therapy happens over the weekend, so I did OT exercises on my own and, with Tony's help, walked around the unit. He and I sat outside a lot on sunny days—I felt it important to get out of the building. We took wheelchair tours of the neighborhood.

I couldn't wait to start the three-hours-per-day inpatient therapy sessions, because each time I worked with the PTs I saw improvement. One of the problems I was having was inverting my right foot, which caused me to trip over my own feet. Because I could neither feel my right foot touching the floor nor control its movement, I could only watch as it strayed about on its own. And, because I couldn't feel when one foot stepped on the other, I frequently tripped. I can remember looking at my right foot and wondering why it was doing what it was doing; my brain was certainly not instructing it to do so (a great example of a proprioception problem). Then, one of my PTs thought to put a four-pound ankle weight on my right foot, and, lo and behold, I could *feel* my foot on floor. Not only that, it behaved better. A simple, elegant solution. PTs are very clever.

The PTs tried to help me use a cane in place of a walker, but I just couldn't find my balance—not yet. I could see in my mind how to do it, but my body wouldn't cooperate. Balance was something we worked on a lot. When I closed my eyes I had absolutely no sense of where I was in space, and I had no balance. No exaggeration. I was (and still am, though to a lesser degree) dependent on my vision to keep my balance. It made me grateful for having good eyesight, as I couldn't imagine how a visually-impaired person would manage. It wasn't until four or five months after surgery that I could close my eyes and keep my balance. I still don't risk it unless I am standing right next to something to grab on to, just in case.

We continued working on going up and down stairs. Here's the thing about stairs: when you feel as if your feet are floating four feet above the ground, stairs are really scary. Over time they became less scary, and soon I could go up and down them, albeit at a sloth-like pace.

DAY FOURTEEN

Any profession is made up of the great, the adequate, and the bad practitioners. I have a good nose for the bad ones, and have zero tolerance for them. Most SCT patients have been through years of misdiagnoses before their tumor is finally found, which means we endure needless suffering at the hands of a lot of inexperienced, but well-meaning, practitioners. That was certainly true for me. Also true is the fact that I would not suffer fools lightly in my recovery. That was how I came to fire a physical therapist.

We were working on mirror therapy, a process whereby you watch yourself in a mirror while doing PT exercises. When you can't feel your body, it's very helpful to watch in a mirror what your body is doing. At the time, my neck rotation was pretty minimal, restricting my ability to look. So there I was, watching myself try to balance on one foot (while holding on to the walker) when my body started shaking. I had no control over it. This sweet, young, inexperienced and thoughtless therapist asked me if I was faking it. I was outraged, I was hurt, and later, I realized that what she really did was shake my confidence in my own experience. I knew I was not "faking it," but somehow having a therapist accuse me of that caused me to doubt my own experience. It is, in my opinion, one of the most disrespectful things staff can do to patients. Fortunately, I had the presence of mind and confidence to speak to her supervisor immediately after that session and ask that I no longer work with that therapist. I think my experience as an RN gave me insight into how medical systems work, and I knew I had the right to ask for another PT. I was very careful to be specific and calm in my complaint against the therapist. I was also clear and firm in my request.

In her defense—even though she worked on a neuro rehab unit—she had never worked with a SCT survivor before. We are very rare patients. She should have known that it was not unusual for patients like me to shake when trying to balance, but she didn't. I could have stuck with her and helped her learn, but I knew that the hours I had in therapy were few and precious, and I had neither the luxury nor the patience to work with anyone less than the best. It was uncomfortable when I saw her everyday in the rehab gym, but, as a result of firing her, I got to work with a great, experienced therapist. I share that story because I hope it gives anyone reading this the courage to walk away from any foolish or ill-equipped novice who is not able to help you in your journey.

DAY FIFTEEN

I wasn't long into the daily therapy sessions when I learned a hard lesson from my over-zealous work ethic.

Here is an excerpt from my Caring Bridge site:

> "Totally crushed it with the cane today!!!!! PT and OT ended up working with me and I walked a lap around the nurse's station using only a cane. So that happened. Feeling pretty darn sassy about it too!"

That sounds like me. "Crushing It" became my battle cry as I charged into therapy each day. I was seeing results. I was exhausted. I was hopeful. I was determined. I was about to be humbled.

It was Christmas Eve. My regular PT and OT therapists were gone for the holiday, and I was to have therapy with a young, well-meaning therapist. Down to the gym we walked. It wasn't my usual gym, and it was twice as far as I usually walked, but I was ready for battle and I toughed it out. When we got there, he set up an obstacle course for me to negotiate. I was eager to try it because, frankly, it looked way more interesting than watching myself balance in a mirror.

I did the course, and then we took the long walk back to my room. I slept awhile, and then Tony took me outside for some fresh air. Suddenly, I completely lost all coordination and balance. I could barely keep myself upright in the wheelchair. Terrified that something horrible was going on, Tony hurried me back to my room. The staff administered a neuro exam that I couldn't pass by any stretch of the imagination.

Here is an excerpt from my Caring Bridge written by Tony:

> "She has had a rough couple of days resulting (we believe) from too much of a good thing—rehab and physical activity. On Thursday, some of the deficits we saw immediately after surgery returned, and it was a bit of a setback. They put her through another 2-hour MRI yesterday to make sure something bad hadn't happened, which was very taxing for her. Worst Christmas Day ever! MRI was normal, thankfully. Today, she is feeling much better and will be taking it easy through the weekend."

Honestly, what I really needed was a nap, not an MRI. Or better yet, I needed the sense to know that the rehab was too advanced. Once again my body was sending me messages in a language I did not understand. That experience was a wake-up call, and the beginning of a new strategy in therapy.

DAY EIGHTEEN

New PT strategy: Not Crushing It.

When my usual PT/OT team returned from the holidays, they were shocked to hear what had happened. My usual approach to therapy was no longer allowed. We learned the hard way that healing from neurosurgery is as much about allowing rest and recovery as it is about work in the rehab gym. Instead of using a pain scale to assess how I was feeling, we would use a fatigue scale. Our new focus was helping me learn to interpret the signals my body was sending.

For example, I experienced fatigue in a different way than before surgery. The new language told me that physical fatigue was setting in when my body started to feel "bigger." (Ten months after surgery and that is still true.) Mental fatigue set in when I began to feel "static" in my brain and became more clumsy and shaky. I was starting to learn the new language. It helped. It made therapy a bit more boring, but it ended up being the most important lesson I learned in my recovery. *Doing* the work was never the issue for me. It was *not* doing the work that was hard. Although I knew that fact going into therapy, I didn't act like it until my body took charge and made me learn the lesson.

Nowadays, when I have a setback, I do a review:
- Am I increasing my walking or bike riding too much?
- Am I working too many hours at my job?
- Am I doing too much physical therapy?
- Did I try a new skill recently? Every time I try to do something I have not done since before surgery (like swimming, biking, etc.), it takes a toll on me, and I need a lot more rest than usual.
- All of the above?
- None of the above?

For the record, at this stage of the game I often put my money on "none of the above." Bad days just seem random.

This I know for sure: I need rest. I'm not just talking about regular naps. I call my naps "Neuro Naps," and they are a different breed of nap altogether. It's not my body that needs the rest, it's my neurological system that needs downtime to process the input it receives.

I've learned the hard way that if I do not give my system a chance to assimilate and integrate a skill that it's relearning, things will turn out badly. When I give my system this time, I never know how long it will take. I can't even estimate. Sometimes it's a five-minute rest, and sometimes it takes days. It appears to be nothing I can think my way through; my body is in charge of this one.

Who would have thought? The experience of recovering from this surgery has nothing at all to do with a "no-pain-no-gain" or "pushing it" kind of attitude. In my view, nothing could be more detrimental. I have come to believe that it's a good life lesson for me in all things, but that is another book.

DAY TWENTY

Living with a SCT means having weird symptoms. Living beyond the surgery means the same. One odd, post-surgical symptom I've had is feeling a twinge, jolt, or strong fluttering sensation every 90 seconds or so. I feel it through the right side of my body, then in my left foot, and then my right hand. It's been happening very predictably in its timing and its pattern every since the surgery, and it still happens today. Luckily, it's not painful. If someone has their hands on me when it happens, they cannot feel it. This surprises me, as it seems strong enough to be seen across a room. It used to drive me nuts, but nowadays I barely notice it. No one seems to know what it is or why I have it, but I do know it's a common experience among the other SCT survivors I have spoken with.

Another symptom I had (and continue to have, but to a lesser degree) is a sensation of tightness in my feet, legs, ribs and right arm. It's called "banding." In my feet it feels like someone is blowing up a blood pressure cuff around my arches and ankles. With my legs it feels like there are thousands of rubber bands tightly wound around them.

Same with my right arm. And around my rib cage it feels like a wide, tight belt is cinched around me. All of these sensations wax and wane, but they are rarely gone completely. I barely notice them when they are subtle, but when they are strong it's impossible to ignore them. As I type this today, the band around my ribs is so tight I find myself intentionally taking calm, deep breaths in order to remember to breathe. As you can imagine, it's hard to do that and complete other tasks at the same time. That's just how it is.

One of the stranger symptoms after surgery was the sensation that my legs were bone-cold freezing. No exaggeration. I felt like I was standing hip-deep in a lake of ice water. It made it hard for me to sleep. The MD Anderson Cancer Center has an Integrative Medicine Department, and, prior to my surgery, I requested a referral to them while in the hospital, so as to take advantage of every service available that might help. They ended up offering me a daily massage. It not only felt good, but it was the only thing that gave me relief from freezing cold legs. A simple, elegant intervention that provided incredible results. My legs are no longer constantly cold, but once again, if am neurologically overwhelmed or overtired, my legs get cold with the kind of cold that blankets can't warm.

I also invited Kundalini Yoga energy healers in to work with me while I was in the hospital. I had visited the Kundalini Yoga Center in Houston prior to my surgery, and was fortunate to meet experienced, supportive teachers and healers. I invited them to visit me in the hospital to help me heal in ways that I knew the medical staff could not offer. I viewed it as an addition to my treatment regimen, not an alternative. Hari Kirn Khalsa (a woman I met through the yoga center) came in the evenings and worked with my body to help heal my nerves. She used Sat Nam Rasayan, an ancient healing art that helped me develop a compassionate awareness of what was happening in my body. It was calming and balancing. I was learning to be present, sensitive, patient, and aware of the multiple factors in play in my healing experience.

There are many, many complimentary therapies available to those of us who have open and curious minds, but you need to find your own balance of inquiry, discernment, and courage when considering them. By accessing both the medical model and the less-traditional models of mind/body awareness and healing, I found a path that has worked for me, and, as a result, I feel I'm having a fantastic outcome. Now that I am home, I continue to use Sat Nam Rasayan in addition to acupuncture, massage and Upper Cervical Chiropractic Care (from a NUCCA certified practitioner). I also benefit from CranioSacral Therapy and Barral Therapy (both from advanced practitioners). I am not giving medical advice. I am just listing the therapies that have helped me the most during the various stages of my healing.

DAY TWENTY-TWO

This would be my last day in the hospital. During my PT session we went outside, where I braved crossing a street, getting in and out of a car, and stepping up and down curbs. I felt overwhelmed, but not too much. It was enough for me to realize that I had been living in a bubble, that the world outside of the hospital was not set up for me, and that it was moving much faster than me. But it was time to leave the hospital, and this time I was ready to go.

We stayed in Houston for three more days. Tony had been living in an apartment while I was in the hospital, so we decided to stay there a few days to give me a trial run at "real life." We had to purchase grab bars and a portable shower chair so I could shower safely at the apartment as well as when we got home. (A number of drugstores, home improvement centers and other places sell quality, "portable" grab bars that are easy to put up and take down.)

Our biggest concern was whether or not I would be able to handle the trip home. Up until this point, I was only able to tolerate being out of bed for a couple of hours at a time. Travel from the hotel to the airport to the plane and to home was going to take at least eight hours.

Before I write about going home, I want to share some of my insights from the hospital bed. There was a particular moment in time after surgery when my attitude toward my body shifted from judgment to gratitude. I remember lying in the hospital bed early one morning, before the staff started coming in to interrupt my day. I was raising my legs in the air, stretching and moving them effortlessly. I began to look at my legs in amazement and wonder. They worked. Despite the fact that the surgeon cut into my spinal cord. Despite the terrifying risk of the surgery paralyzing me. Despite the possibility that my legs would be too weak or uncoordinated to carry me. They worked. Suddenly I realized, that for the first time since I was fifteen, I loved my legs. They were no longer too fat, too hairy, too short, too anything. I was in love with my legs. I bowed to them in gratitude and amazement for their willingness to function so perfectly despite the surgery. I was no longer angry with my body for growing a tumor. The tumor was gone, and my body remained functional. A stalwart ally. I began to consider every part of my body in the same way and felt full of gratitude. It has been, for me, a return to loving my body. A break from judgment. A relief.

A year before I had surgery, I was a person who felt like I might just go over a cliff. This surprised me, as I had always considered myself a competent, confident person capable of handling difficult situations. But, as the SCT symptoms became harder to deny and the surgery seemed more inevitable, I found myself obsessing with thoughts of the tumor, and the decision of whether or not to risk the surgery. It was ruining the quality of my life.

I started searching for a way to change my life, so I would be prepared to stand firm on the cliff of surgery and face its unknown outcome. This decision about surgery was the most difficult one I've ever made. What if the outcome of the surgery was bad and I couldn't get over the regret of having made the wrong decision? What if I had waited too long to have the surgery, and the outcome turned out to be worse because of my delay? Why couldn't I do anything to make the tumor go away? How could I find the secret to living well with a tumor? If I decided to have the surgery, would I be able to maneuver gracefully through the recovery?

For me, the answer was (and still is) Kundalini Yoga. I found it "accidentally" while attending a Gentle Yoga class and ending up in a teacher/student relationship with Kathryn Gonzalez, a Kundalini teacher. Kathryn showed up in my life at the perfect time, and with the perfect set of tools that I needed, to get through this thing. I knew now that I would not only be able to stand on the edge of the cliff, but I would do so gracefully solid.

Kundalini is a practice of yoga that engages the nerves and makes them function better (a good idea for someone with a central nervous system tumor). Sat Kartar Khalsa (another teacher from the yoga center) helped me understand this better when he told me that in the practice of Kundalini Yoga, we ask our body and mind to simultaneously come into a certain posture, a mental focus, and a breath rhythm. The effect of these actions is to stimulate the nervous system, and to develop strength in muscles and nerves. During the rest period following the exercise, the system is allowed to relax, resulting in enhanced function and a greater ability to tolerate stress. Interesting, isn't it, that yoga teaches us that our nervous system needs to rest in between activities. Just the lesson I needed to learn.

Kathryn told me that yoga is a means of preparing to be our best self in our daily life. It is because of my daily yoga practice that I know what it feels like to be solid, grounded, rooted, and calm. Now, when life starts to knock me around and I get off balance, I recognize that this is not who I am, nor who I want to be. I know how to handle these situations in a solid manner because, each day, I practice being solid.

I did yoga each day in my hospital bed, because I wasn't able to get down to the floor by myself. Even if I could get to the floor, there wasn't a chance I'd be able to get back up. So I'd put the side rails up on my bed and do my yoga. If I couldn't sit up, I would do it lying down. It's what kept me steady.

DAY TWENTY-SIX

After 35 days in Houston, it was time to go home to northern Minnesota. We planned well for the trip home. We stayed at the hotel attached to the airport to lessen the travel time. We arranged for a wheelchair from the hotel to the airport, and then another wheelchair once in the airport. I was in no shape to walk very far at this point, and I knew that fatigue management was a priority. We decided on the financial indulgence of flying first class so I could be more comfortable. We arranged for wheelchair assistance in the connecting airport. The airport traveler assistance office at the Minneapolis airport arranged a place for me to lie down during our three-hour layover. All of these things helped immensely and the trip went so much better than we anticipated. Best of all was being surprised by a group of my friends at my home airport, who greeted me with roses and hugs. When I got home, there was a huge banner hanging in front of our house welcoming us back. I have the best friends ever.

I referred to the people in my support system as "Sherpas." Few people risk climbing Mt. Everest without the support of Sherpas. This was my Everest. There was no underestimating my need, nor my gratitude, for the Sherpas in the hospital and at home. Those that lived close by made meals and organized a schedule of drivers to get me to and from appointments (it was two months before I was able to drive). Sherpas that did not live close by supported me with their prayers, meditations, positive vibes, or whatever spiritual support they chose to offer. There were others who supported us with their financial donations, which we needed. I honored all of it, and all of it helped.

A word about finances, being sick is expensive. We flew from Minnesota to Houston for appointments and surgery. We were in Houston for 35 days. Expenses included an apartment rental for Tony (and the others who came to help), a car rental, parking (a surprisingly large sum), plane tickets, meals, pet care, and more. We used GoFundMe, a user-friendly online fundraising site, and were blessed with donations that allowed us to go through this difficult time without the burden of financial concerns. It was a hard decision to accept donations (not to mention an ego check), but then, we learned to accept a lot of hard things on our journey through this.

People wanted to know how they could help. When asked, I would refer them to the GoFundMe web page, but also told them that an equally valued gift would be that they pray/meditate/ask the following, along with me, for all those who touch me with their care during this time:

- That they bring their best skill, clarity, creativity and partnership to the exchange, for the best outcome.
- That their personal lives and work lives be full, peaceful and happy in between the times that they connect with me. That way we can all benefit from our interactions.

TWO MONTHS

I was two months post-op, and had been home for one month. I was well cared for. My Sherpas schlepped me from appointment to appointment with welcome conversation and happy dispositions. Delicious food and cheerful flowers showed up at my door. Family and friends remained stalwart supporters of my recovery. I was grateful.

I had OT twice per week. While working on improving the fine motor skills in my right hand, we discovered that wearing a compression glove allowed me to complete fine motor tasks *and* increased the speed of those tasks by 30%. Hard data. This meant I was able to drive better and write better (I could finally read my own handwriting, though it still did not look normal). Typing was easier than writing, but both tasks caused surprising fatigue.

With that success in mind we tried compression socks—it made a huge difference in how well I could feel my feet. This not only meant I could work my car's gas/brake pedals better, it also meant I stopped tripping over my own feet. I wish we had tried compression gear right after surgery, as it would have been interesting to see if I would have improved more quickly. The way I understand compression is that it helps the brain remember that the hand or foot is *there*, that it *exists*, and it worked great for me. I don't need to use them anymore, as now I can feel the gas/brake pedals. I can type. I can write. I'm getting better all the time.

I had PT three times per week, and we had hard data that showed my endurance, balance and coordination were improving. I ditched the quad cane and used a single-point cane when walking outside. I no longer needed a cane in the house, and that made life more manageable. My stride was smoother, and I didn't look so stiff when I walked.

Sensory-wise, things were changing. It felt as though parts of my body were "thawing out." I was very itchy in my feet, the back of my head, and my ribs. I interpreted this as nerve changes. Although I remained numb from the knee down in my left leg, and from the chest down on right side of body, the front of my right leg was feeling less numb. And, as my ribs "thawed out" on my right side, I was extremely ticklish—weird, but true.

Life during recovery was very slow. My days consisted of activity balanced with rest. Showering and dressing tired me more than anything and took up half my day. I felt fatigue after any and all activity, and I honored that fatigue with naps. (*Naps! Naps! Naps!* was my warrior cry.) I was able to go up and down my stairs at this point, and that made dealing with my doggies much easier. I tried to do a bit of housework each day. Reading was difficult because of the strain it put on my neck (which was still stiff) so I binge-watched TV instead. Through all of this, I continued my daily yoga and meditation practice.

A bit of advice here about footwear. Two words: flat and laced. Ever since my surgery I've felt as if there was something between my feet and the floor, like an air cushion, or a tennis ball, or a pile of marshmallows. The more surface contact I have with the floor, the easier it is to keep my balance, and the less work my brain has to do to keep me upright. Tony found a type of shoe from Merrell, called Vapor Glove, that mimics the feel of being barefoot. They worked great in Houston, but now we were home in northern Minnesota in January and I needed boots. My usual winter footwear had thick soles for winter, but the higher my foot is from the floor the more it feels like I am hovering instead of walking. We found mukluks worked the best. They are incredibly warm, look cool, and have a thinner flexible sole. Now that I am ten months out from surgery, I find I can wear tennis shoes, which is as high off the ground as I can tolerate. Thick-soled shoes and boots are still too much for me.

I learned the hard way that I needed to have shoes that lace up, because it is super easy for me to just walk right out of my shoes and not know it. Six months after surgery, I was in the Denver airport wearing a pair of slip-on shoes (similar to espadrilles) and I walked half the length of a concourse before I realized I was only wearing one shoe! I turned around and walked back, searching for my other shoe. There is no way to look cool when you find your shoe in the middle of the concourse and put it back on your foot, pretending like it was something you had intended to do.

My knees still felt weird, like there were tennis balls where my knees should be. When I was on my knees, it felt all squishy and round. It was incredibly challenging to be on my hands and knees, or to balance on my knees. The same was true for lying on my stomach. I felt like I was hovering over the ground; I simply did not feel my body in contact with the floor. These were positions I practiced in yoga. I can't say that my practice changed the way things felt, but it did give me more confidence, making me more comfortable in the discomfort.

Getting "comfortable in the discomfort" is very much what this whole recovery has been like. My life's challenge is learning to be okay with my post-surgery symptoms, and I would not describe it as a process that I can *think* my way through. I have to consistently practice doing things that are challenging without labeling them, so I can come to a place in my mind where I can be content in the mystery – the mystery of not knowing the degree to which my body will recover, the mystery of not knowing if I will live the rest of my life never feeling what my skin touches in the same way I felt it before. Sometimes I feel so full of grief for what I've lost. Sometimes I feel quite content in my new situation. Sometimes I'm pissed as hell that this ever happened to me. And sometimes I feel quite content in my new situation.

It's been a weird journey, but I'd managed to remain grateful. It seemed like the hardest stuff was in my rear view mirror. The headache was gone. The tumor was gone. My life felt full, like there was nothing but adventure ahead.

THREE MONTHS

We reached a big milestone in OT: I was able to close my eyes and feel objects that were placed in my right hand. I could also finally feel someone touching my fingers and toes on my right hand and foot. It was a big deal for me. Meeting measurable goals was satisfying.

I had PT/OT twice weekly and hoped to drop that to once weekly, as I wanted to exchange indoor therapy with more time in the woods with my dogs. I was easily managing a mile walk in the woods each day. There were days that I could walk two miles, and days that I couldn't. I was driving routinely now, and that made me more independent and social, which helped my state of mind. I was surprised to find that the hardest part of driving was getting a sore and tired neck—I thought it would be something like not feeling the gas and brake pedals (which turned out not to be so bad). The neck soreness got better over time, but at ten months it is still the limiting factor in how far I can tolerate driving. The farthest I have driven so far is six hours. Not bad.

Many people have asked me what my numbness feels like. Imagine that you are wearing a fuzzy, soft glove and someone touches your glove-covered index finger. You can feel them touching the *glove*, but you can't feel them touching your actual *finger*. That is how the numb parts of my body feel. It's as if there is a fuzzy force field around me, and although I no longer feel actual touch, I do have a sense that someone has entered the fuzzy force field around my body.

Here is another way to describe it. You know how your lip feels after getting novocaine? It *feels* huge, but when you look in the mirror you can see that it's normal. That is how my butt and legs feel most of the time. When parts of my body started to "thaw" they got itchy, but it's not an itch you can scratch. The itching was usually followed by an extreme burning sensation, then, a little less numbness in that part of the body. Another part of the language I had to learn: numbness followed by itching followed by burning equals less numbness. I reminded myself that this "thawing" was another process my body was going through, that the symptoms were temporary, and that the end result would be some kind of a change. These thoughts helped me get through the sensations, especially the extreme burning part. It's a good example of how my rule not to label things as *good* or *bad* was useful.

FOUR MONTHS

I made a trip to Florida to visit my parents and was able to travel solo, which felt like a big accomplishment. I used a wheelchair in the airport as a part of my fatigue management plan. Yes, I could have made the long walk in the airport without it, but that could have resulted in my being too tired to enjoy the trip, so I swallowed my ego and used the wheelchair.

It was here I learned some lessons from swimming. Therapy at home had been going well. The PTs were encouraging me to start using pool therapy, so I thought I would start it in Florida. Naively, I did not ask for guidance on what exactly I was to *do* for pool therapy.

It was an 86-degree day when my parents and I headed to the pool. I've always been a strong swimmer, so I figured I would just, well, start swimming. Right away I realized that this was going to be a big deal for my body. I still could not feel my legs (I needed to look at them to know they were there), but when I walked into that pool,

I *knew* I had legs, because the pressure of the water surrounding them triggered my brain to remember. Remarkable.

At that point I should have turned around, walked out of the pool, and rested. But I figured if a little stimulation is good, then a lot is better, so I started swimming. I was in the pool for about eight minutes when my brain informed me that it was on overload and it was time to get out, so I did, only to find out I couldn't walk. My brain was too overwhelmed. My parents helped me to a chair and I immediately fell asleep. After three hours they finally woke me and helped me back to their home, where I slept for most of 24 hours. It took over a week to fully recover.

Two weeks after that trip, I flew solo to Houston for my return visit to see the neurosurgeon at MD Anderson. This time I managed the trip without a wheelchair. I was feeling great when I arrived, in a whole new state of mind and health. My previous visits to MD Anderson were stressful. I always felt anxious in that building, no doubt because most everyone you see at this clinic is fighting an epic battle. I knew it to be a populace of strong, brave, vulnerable people, but this time I was not one of them. This time I felt like a success story. A victor. My neurosurgeon was pleased with my progress, as I knew he would be. It was great.

At home, I was trying my hand at getting back to work at the hospital. I started with one four-hour shift each week, which was exhausting. Socially it was fun, but the duties were challenging. My right hand did not want to cooperate, so each task I did with patients took a really long time, and made me nervous, a feeling I hadn't had since I was a brand new nurse. It was humbling to struggle with things that at one time had come so naturally, and every time I did I was brought face-to-face with my disability. That was the hardest part. I had a problem admitting I had a disability, even though I was careful not to see it as a label as much as a fact. Although I dislike it, some things don't change just because you don't want to admit they're real. I am learning to look at things more honestly and less shaded by my desire for them to be different.

SIX MONTHS

I was still numb from my chest to my toes on the right side of the body, and from knee to toes on the left side. My whole backside was numb. The numbness had changed a lot in the sense that I was less numb every day. However, it was still pretty impressive numbness. More impressive was my body's ability to function even when I didn't feel like I had a body. I wish I could explain that better, but I can't. There are precious few SCT survivors out there, and those I speak with are the only people who can grasp how weird this is.

I'll try to give some examples. I rely a great deal on my eyesight and hearing to maneuver safely. For example, I tap my feet against things I can't feel, so I can hear where my feet are in relation to other objects. I still have to look at what is in my right hand in order to use it properly and safely. I still have to check to be sure I actually have clothes on because fabric and skin feels pretty much the same to me, though that has been changing for the better. My socks and slippers come off frequently without my knowing it, and I tend to walk out of my shoes.

I was doing well enough with gross motor skills (walking, feeding myself, dressing myself, and so on) that I "graduated" out of OT. I could type with relative ease and speed. I was driving. My handwriting was not only legible, I actually recognized it as my own. I still went to PT twice a week, where I was relearning how to skip, swim, ride a bike, and improve my balance.

Whenever I was confronted with relearning a skill, I found I was clumsy. It was confusing and exhausting, even though it seemed like it should be so easy. After some work, patience, and a good sense of humor, however, the wires would suddenly just reconnect. Once that happened, I totally "had it," and I was ready to start working on the next skill. Both my PTs and I found it downright fascinating to observe this process. I can tell you it gave me insight, empathy, and glacial patience for anyone I encounter who has a neurological injury. I know each task is much harder than it appears.

Although my activity tolerance was much better (I managed a two-mile walk each day) I was still exhausted each evening and, on most days, I needed an afternoon nap. I continued a daily Kundalini yoga and meditation practice, to which I credit a great deal of my healing. I had a goal to ride a bike outdoors by the end of summer—a lofty aim considering I was just relearning how to ride on an indoor stationary bike.

I soon moved on to a three-wheel bike (which at first was both tragedy *and* comedy), and once I figured that out, I moved up to a regular bike. I really thought that once I could ride a bike, I would be able to ride for at least as long a time as I could walk. But, by the end of the summer, I could still only tolerate ten minutes on the bike no matter how much I tried to gain increased tolerance. There was just something about riding a bike that made my legs spasm and get too stiff to continue. It also made me extremely neurologically fatigued. Maybe next year.

Fortunately, I was celebrating a lot of improvements during this month. I went to Colorado to be with my friend for her surgery. While there, I hiked two miles at a 7,500-foot elevation. Tony and I went to see a concert that involved a four-hour drive. We booked a hotel within walking distance from the arena so that I could more easily leave the concert if I couldn't handle it. I was worried about safely walking in crowds in the dark, and about walking on bleachers. I sat down a lot to rest, but we did it, and I had a really good time. Things were looking up.

Throughout my progress I remained amazed at my body and its ability to relearn skills and adapt to new ways of completing tasks. I was a bit slower than I used to be, and I was loath to use the phrase "new normal," even though it applied. I was continuing to figure out the balance between rest and activity. I call to mind a great quote from poet David Whyte: "Rest is the conversation between what we want to do and how we want to be." It's pointless to push myself to do more when I'm fatigued; I just get more and more clumsy, lose fine motor control, rev up my sensory symptoms, and then it all falls apart. That is not how I want to be, so I continue to embrace rest.

EIGHT MONTHS

I was about to learn the hard way that the numb parts of my body don't experience pain the same way they used to. More language lessons from my body.

We went to see a Wilco concert (my favorite band). It was a trip that involved a three-hour drive and camping. At the concert, the crowd was dancing and jumping, and I just had to join in. I was amazed that I could do it. I remember telling Tony that jumping is really fun when it feels like there are tennis balls and air pockets between your feet and the ground. It was a lovely summer evening, and I was having a blast. It didn't occur to me that I was 51 years old and maybe should have known better than to jump around. After the concert, I noticed I was having trouble putting weight on my right foot. It didn't hurt, but it did feel weak and unstable. An hour or so later, I was unable to bear any weight on the foot at all. It was a bad ankle sprain, and I was embarrassed that I did this to myself, though I was amazed that it didn't hurt at all during the concert. Okay, another lesson learned: if you don't have feeling in your feet and ankles, you won't be able to tell if they are being injured.

August had been an epic month of accomplishing goals, but at the end of the month I had a weird setback. In the middle of a normal day, the room suddenly began to spin and I felt really unwell. In an instant I felt weak all over and realized I didn't have enough balance to get off the couch. I told Tony, and we decided to wait it out to see if it resolved. I went back to using a cane and needed assistance to walk. It was scary. I felt awful. When I woke up the next morning I was still in bad shape, so, on the advice of my neuro team, I went to the ER and had an MRI. It was normal. They wanted to admit me into the hospital, but honestly, I couldn't see the point, so we went home. Over the next days and weeks my symptoms slowly resolved. I refrained from going to work for one month after that, wanting to see if more rest would prevent a recurrence. I rested more than usual and consulted with my care teams. No one knew what had happened, and no one knew what to do about it. It would seem my body just had to figure these things out over time.

I've had other odd symptoms, rough days, and setbacks along the journey. It seems to follow somewhat of a cycle. I have a few spectacular weeks, followed by something going wrong, followed by my body seeming to find its own way back to recovery. I am unable to *think* my way to a healthy state again; it just takes time. That is difficult for me, as I prefer to figure out cause and effect, develop a strategy for avoiding recurrence of symptoms, and proceed with a plan of recovery. That process doesn't work anymore. At least, not so far.

When odd symptoms pop up, there are those who jump to the conclusion that I've been overdoing it. Yes, I know I'm inclined to overdo things from time to time, and I know it causes my neuro system to overload and not work well. I'm all too familiar with what that feels like. But there are other circumstances that are more mysterious. I've experimented with doing too little and doing too much, and I've had setbacks occur during each. There is no cause-and-effect pattern; it's just not that clear cut. From my experiences, I've come to believe that our central nervous systems are meticulously interwoven with everything inside *and* outside our bodies. It's delicate, it likes balance. Unfortunately, it's not very well understood. It seems it doesn't take much to upset the balance in me, and, when it's out-of-whack, I'm affected in ways I don't understand. I am still learning that part of the new language.

Some things do cause exacerbation of symptoms. Things like a falling barometer. When a storm is coming, my nerves are busier (for lack of a better term) than usual. When I am fighting a virus or an illness, I notice that my central nervous system is more affected, resulting in a feeling of being "big" all over and a worsening of my sensory symptoms, including balance. There isn't much to be done about these situations except to understand and accept that on those days I probably won't get my errands run, my walk will be shorter, and a meal may not get made. These things are hard for me to take (remember my damn work ethic) but I've finally come to a place where I can say that this is how it is for now. It's best to accept that pushing it during these times inevitably causes everything to get worse.

I am realizing at this stage of the recovery that, for the first time in my life, I can't make something better by sheer willpower. It's a hard lesson, and I'm learning it over and over. I'm continually challenged to deepen my understanding of what my mind's role is in this recovery. Once again, I come back to the idea of how our culture admires, praises and rewards those who strive after goals and succeed. For me, it simply doesn't work like that.

Striving is the old way. I am learning a new way—a way of acceptance. Patience. Reconciling expectations with reality. Of course I have disappointments and longings. I wish I could feel my feet on the ground in the same way I did before surgery. I wish I could feel the outline of my body more distinctly. I wish I could feel my butt resting on the cushion of the chair I'm sitting on. I wish I had more energy. I wish the healing experience was more predictably good and the bad days were fewer.

It's like planting a tree. All I can do is provide an environment in which a young tree would be able to grow. I plant it in rich soil and provide water and sunlight, but I don't make the tree grow. The tree does that. This stage of my recovery feels similar. I am doing my therapy. I am resting. I exercise. I remain curious. I take care of my mind and my spirit. But I am not in charge of how my central nervous system is healing. I can't speed up my healing any more than I could speed up a growing tree. Trust me, I've tried. It doesn't work that way.

TEN MONTHS

I tried lymphatic drainage therapy from a certified lymph drainage therapist, and after that I got a lot of feeling back in my feet—more feeling than I had a few months ago. I could feel my socks on my feet, and I don't walk out of my shoes anymore. We are still in a quandary about whether to continue the therapy or not. In some ways I feel better after the therapy, but in some ways I feel worse. There is a lymphatic system in the central nervous system that is not well understood, and I think we're sometimes aggravating it and causing new symptoms, while at the same time we're relieving sensory symptoms. So many things to discover. So many things to be curious about.

I am still numb from my collarbone to my toes on the right side of my body and from my knee to my toes on the left side. However the numbness is less intense than it was. It has changed over time for the better. The left side of my body works so much better than it did before surgery. The right side, however, is another story. As I sit here typing, I realize I am using all of my fingers quite easily. Much improved. I can put in my own earrings in now (a delicate task for fine motor skills). I drive without any trouble. I walk three miles most days. I don't stumble on uneven ground or need a cane like I did before surgery. As I write this I am reminded of how much I have taken for granted. How far I've come. How I've lost that sense of profound gratitude I felt when I first woke up and realized I had survived the surgery.

I am trying to work between 8–12 hours each week at the hospital. I had really hoped to be up to 20 hours per week at work by now, but I am clearly not in charge of how fast this recovery happens. For now, I hope to maintain the 8–12 hours until I feel it's safe to increase that. I also own a small business (an online retail store that sells supplies to fiber artists) and I am able to work from home each day in the business.

Hindsight is 20/20. As I write about my experience ten months after surgery, I realize that I do not have the benefit of hindsight; I am still in the midst of the experience. What I know for sure is that the changes I experience now are not as exciting, impressive, or rapid as those I experienced in the weeks just after surgery. This is the "drudgery of recovery." My new perspective on recovery is to have a steadfast regimen of therapy that cultivates my continued improvement, while at the same time find a path that accepts my life as forever altered because of the surgery. But then, getting a tumor in your spinal cord means your life is forever altered whether you have the surgery or not.

I sometimes think I should have had the surgery sooner. Maybe the tumor would have been smaller and wouldn't have attached itself to the right side of the cord, resulting in fewer adverse reactions on the right side of my body. But early on, when the tumor was small, my symptoms were more tolerable, so I would have postponed the surgery anyway, and so on. I try not to dwell on this. I did the best I could in making the hardest decision of my life about when to have the surgery. I've never regretted having the surgery. *As hard as this recovery has been, I am better than I was before the surgery.*

This is a good time to list the things are better since the surgery:

- My relentless, untreatable three-year headache is gone; the headaches I get now are intermittent and treatable.
- The pain in my left leg and foot is gone. Since about a year before surgery, I was having as much pain in my left leg and foot as I had in my head. It was wearing me out.
- My need for a cane is gone. Before surgery I was using a cane when I walked on uneven surfaces because my left leg would drag, sometimes causing me to stumble and risk falling.
- The dizziness and vertigo I had for years is gone. Those symptoms were not well understood by my medical team; another example of the mystery of the central nervous system. I always had a feeling that they were tumor-related. I had tried everything else to cure them and nothing worked—except the surgery.
- The pins-and-needles sensation I had in my hands and feet is gone.
- I no longer get electrical shocks shooting through my arms when I turn my head.
- Before surgery, I was having trouble sensing when my bladder was full. I would schedule a trip to the bathroom every two hours because, if I didn't, I would sometimes find my bladder to be absolutely full without my knowing it. Thankfully, I was always

continent, but I also knew that the longer I let this symptom continue, the less chance I would have of maintaining continence. Since my surgery, I no longer have a problem sensing when I have to urinate, and I no longer schedule bathroom trips every two hours.

- I no longer have the stress linked to making a decision about the "if" and "when" of my surgery.
- I no longer have the stress linked to wondering if it was the tumor that was causing so many of my symptoms, because now the tumor is gone.

My life feels more hopeful now. Before surgery, I was in slow decline and the future was uncertain and scary. Now the future looks hopeful.

Before surgery, my neurosurgeon cautioned me that "surgery will not be a free lunch," and he was right. I had a beautiful surgical outcome, but found I traded in old symptoms for new challenges. The damage to my right hand has been the most frustrating outcome. If you were to look at me now, ten months post-op, you would never know I had the surgery. Considering what might have happened, I think a frustrating problem with my right hand is a small thing. That doesn't mean I don't cuss a bit when I fumble with tasks—I figure I'm entitled.

I have increased fatigue, which, although it's improved, I had hoped it would be better by now. I've read about people whose tumors were lower on the spine than mine was, and they are out running marathons and climbing mountains and working full time within a year of having surgery. Clearly, that wasn't my experience. It could be that a high cervical tumor like mine involves a more difficult recovery, I don't really know. I do know that I feel I've had a spectacular recovery, even though I'm more limited than others in the scope of my activities.

I continue to struggle to "speak the language" of my post-surgical body. The hardest thing for me since surgery has been figuring out the line between comfortably pushing myself and overdoing it. It's strange, because when I am meeting goals and moving on with life, people around me cheer and applaud me for my fortitude and hard work. As soon as I have a setback or look tired, those same people are quick to blame it on my overdoing it. I've come to believe that blaming every unpleasant outcome on "overdoing it" is a lazy conclusion, and that I can trust my intuition about whether I am overdoing it or not. Presumably, my fatigue will lessen over the years, I'll have to wait and see. For now, it's an opportunity to practice reconciling expectations with reality.

Learning to live in a body that feels completely different is hard. I've lived in this body for 51 years, and to be suddenly dropped into a body that feels different, acts different, and speaks a whole new language, has daily challenges.

There are days when my symptoms rear their ugly heads and everything is hard to do. My body doesn't cooperate, and it's a struggle. On those days I am sometimes fearful that I've reached the end of my recovery and things may never get any better than this. Not a good place to be. I know better. I know that being present in the immediate experience is the key to surviving those thoughts. I *know* that, but I still go there sometimes.

Fortunately, most days I feel good, and my body cooperates with me in a way I want it to. On those days, life is really great and hopeful, and I barely think about the surgery or the recovery process.

As I write this, I am coming up on the first-year anniversary of my surgery. This is how I see it: I had a tumor. I had the surgery. The tumor is gone. I've done the best I could with what I was given. Maybe I *am* a rock star.

AFTERWORD

The one-year anniversary of the surgery has now come and gone. The latest MRI shows that the tumor is gone (yay!) and the surgical site is healing beautifully.

When I wrote *ReWired*, I intended that it cover just the first ten months of my surgical recovery. But something has shifted in the last two months, and I felt it was too important—and hopeful—to leave out. What I want to tell you is that it keeps getting better. This recovery, this healing, continues to happen.

At the end of ten months, things were still kind of rough for me, and it felt like I was ending the book on a melancholy note. In the last month, however, my recovery turned a corner for the better. I am working more hours at my job at the hospital. I am doing more fun things because I have the energy to do them. I am cross-country skiing again, one of my favorite winter activities.

Think about that for a minute—three months ago I could only ride a bike for ten minutes, and that was after I spent two months relearning how to ride it. We had our first decent snowfall of the season last week, so I decided to try skiing. Unlike my experiences with swimming and biking, I found I was able to ski without first having to relearn it. In fact, I skied as far, as fast, and as well as I had before the tumor diagnosis. I have to tell you that I was smiling so much during the ski that I got a "brain freeze" headache from the cold air swirling around in my sinuses!

This is important—*healing continues*. It keeps getting better. *I* keep getting better. One evening last week, while I was sitting on the couch, I suddenly realized that my body felt completely normal. I didn't have zinging sensations in my legs, no ball under my butt! No tight bands around my body. It was relaxing. It was hopeful. It was glorious. I told my husband, "I feel *normal*, like I didn't have surgery." Then I sat on the couch and smiled for an hour. *Wow*. If it can happen for an hour, it can happen again—and maybe for longer.

I wrote this book with the following specific intentions:

1) That anyone affected by a spinal cord tumor diagnosis would find their way to this book, and that they would find the book helpful in alleviating some of the fears of the unknown that surround the diagnosis and surgical experience.

2) That medical teams working with SCT patients would gain a new perspective and understanding of the patient experience.

3) That medical teams would offer this book to SCT patients when they are asked for more information about the surgical experience.

4) That I would be better able to not only understand my own surgical recovery experience, but also be able to put that experience in my rearview mirror.

I believe I accomplished those goals. Writing this book *has* helped me put the experience in my rearview mirror. In fact, I find I don't think about it that much anymore. I am living my life again in a fuller, more familiar way. Better now than in the past ten months. Better now than in the past few years, actually.

I know that I would have liked a book like this when I was preparing for surgery. It likely would have given me equal doses of fear and hope. I give it to you now with the prayer that it helps you on your journey, whether you are living with a spinal cord tumor, loving someone who has one, or treating someone with one.

APPENDIX

6th Annual Spine Tumor Patient Education Conference:
When is Surgery Right for Me?
http://tinyurl.com/DawnStandera

What follows is the transcript from Dawn Standera's presentation at the 2015 Spinal Tumor Patient Education Conference at the MD Anderson Cancer Center. The talk not only chronicles Dawn's five-year journey of coping with the tumor and its symptoms, it also highlights her insights into the unique and difficult decision faced by spinal cord tumor patients about whether or not to have tumor-removal surgery.

I am here to talk about what it is like to live with a spinal cord tumor and the difficult decision of when to have surgery to remove the tumor.

Since finding out about the tumor in 2011 I have wanted to talk to people in the same situation. So this conference seemed like the perfect place to talk about it in hopes that I accomplish a few things:

1) That it connects people living with spinal cord tumors so that we will all feel less alone

2) For most of the years since I've known about the tumor I haven't talked about it openly because of a few reasons:

I'm afraid that it will look like I want pity

I'm afraid to bum people out.

I've been an ER nurse for eleven years and ER nurses tend to not tolerate whiners well. I didn't want to be seen as a whiner and I was concerned that if I talked about my symptoms it would look like I was using them as an excuse so I've been pretending that the symptoms don't bother me very much. However, I've recently decided that it is not healthy way to live. So here I am talking about it because like it or not it's a huge part of who I am.

My tumor is likely an ependymoma. It measures 1.6 cm x 9 mm x 9 mm and is located inside the spinal cord at the level of C1-C2, which is very high in the spinal cord and the higher the tumor the higher the risk for more damage from the surgery.

So for the past four years I have made the decision to live with the tumor. The hardest decision I will ever have to make in my life is a decision I have to make every single day and that is this, How will I know when it is the right time to have surgery to take out the tumor?

Here is my story:

In 2011 I woke up from a nap before going to work a night shift in the ER. When I woke up I knew something was wrong with me and I proceeded to have a seizure like episode. I ended up in the ER as a patient where I was worked up, they found nothing wrong and I stayed the night in the ICU. The next morning I got out of bed and fell down which bought me an MRI of my head which caught an image of something in my spinal cord. Long story short, the seizures ended up being secondary to Lyme's Disease and were not caused by the tumor. But having that MRI began my journey of living with the knowledge that I have a spinal cord tumor in a really dangerous location.

After that I had lots of MRIs, tests, consults. I had lots of bad information. Most of the doctors I saw had never had a patient with a C2 tumor and did not know what to do with me. I often felt like doctors were playing the "Not it Game" with me which meant I was kicked around from one specialist to another without anyone helping me to understand my symptoms, without anyone helping me manage my symptoms and certainly without consistent advice about what to do or not do about the tumor.

I was symptom free for a couple years. I mean, I guess I can look back and see that there were weird symptoms that I could correlate to the tumor, but they were intermittent and hard to describe. Then I started having daily weird symptoms that my neurological medical team dismissed as not making sense to them. After many frustrating months of trying to get some help with symptoms and failing I finally fired them and went looking for someone better. My sister in law suggested I look at

MD Anderson and so I got on the website and found the videos from the spinal tumor patient education conferences. I received more information watching those videos than I found in four years of being treated at what is generally regarded as a top notch medical institution. So I sought out a second opinion from Dr. Rhines and Gisela. After our first consultation my husband and I knew this was our team. For the first time we received helpful information, were taken seriously and felt like we were in experienced hands. Once I found medical safety, my anxiety level dropped.

Our basic need as humans is to feel safe. How could I make wise decisions in a medical environment in which I did not feel safe? My best advice to anyone seeking care for a spinal cord tumor is to find the team that is right for you. And fire the teams that are not right for you.

But it's harder than it sounds.

Searching for that medical team often results in a kind of medical loneliness and hopelessness. And it takes a lot of work to find the right team and cruelly it means that you have to find that team at a time when your symptoms are likely bad enough to make you seek help and your loneliness is at a height, you are frustrated and tired and scared and you just don't feel good. Don't even get me started about insurance companies and the roadblocks they put in our way! But it's worth it to fight that fight because as I said before – we cannot make wise decisions and we cannot heal if we are in a medical environment in which we do not feel safe.

Okay, so let's talk symptoms and I think it's important to do for a few reasons (now remember I'm not allowed to be a whiner so this isn't that easy for me to do) but when I talk to other people who have the same symptoms that I do I feel less crazy and alone. And it is amazing to hear the similarity of symptoms among other people with tumors in the same location.

Also, because symptoms that are related to spinal cord tumors are often not obvious, we struggle in ways that are not obvious. By that I mean that people don't see the weird sensations that the tumor causes, so on the surface I look perfectly normal. In some ways it's great that people don't see the symptoms so I can look perfectly normal. And that can be lonely. Think about it – when you break your arm people see the cast and know you are impaired because of it. But people don't see pins and needles and electrical shocks that shoot through our arms and legs so they don't know how tiring it can be to live with these symptoms.

I also think it's important to talk about symptoms because every time a new symptom pops up it begs the question, "Is this the symptom that means it is time to have surgery?" Because every new symptom has to be considered and it can drive you crazy trying to figure out if it is tumor related or if it is related to something that can be fixed or managed which means I can put off surgery longer.

Here we go with symptoms:

It's been a progression that started with pins and needles in my feet, seemed like that was worse in the morning when I got out of bed. It used to come and go but for the past three years it has been constant and slowly moving up my legs so that now I have that weird pins/needles/numb feeling from my feet to mid thigh. Oh, and most recently I have a buzzing/vibration feeling in my legs.

I have the same feeling in my hands. Right arm is worse than the left but the general pins/needles/numb feeling is now from my fingers to just below my shoulders. Now that weird feeling is in my lower rib cage – that just showed up this past summer. I also have balance problems when I turn my head in certain positions. Then there was that year and a half when I couldn't use my left arm properly – but that's a long story!

The worse symptom that I have is nerve pain across the back of my head. It started at the base of my skull. Over the past three years it spread up my head and kind of covers the whole back of my head. And it's very, very intense behind my ears. And it never goes away.

I get breaks with medication use; maybe an hour or two in the mid morning and mid day if I'm lucky. We have tried many interventions at the pain management clinic here. Unfortunately they haven't worked long term, but at least we've tried them. Where I was before they told me there is no way the pain is related to the tumor therefore they couldn't help me – all of which just made me feel crazy and left me with a bad headache. At least here I was taken seriously and I have worked closely with the pain management team who really tried to help, but it seems the only possible solution is surgery – which, of course, may or may not work and may bring more problems than a headache. Although honestly, having a headache for three years is GETTING OLD!

Finally I have days that I call "Storm Days" where it seems like my whole central nervous system is irritated. I get electrical currents showering down my whole body, my head aches, my legs burn and vibrate and on those days my symptoms change from sensory to motor. I often need a cane for balance. My left foot drags and I catch it on the floor and stumble. Thank goodness the motor problems are intermittent. I wish I knew what causes storm days, but I don't. They are very unpredictable.

Because of the unpredictable nature of storm days I have almost completely stopped working. I work very part time in Interventional Radiology but my career as an ER nurse is over. I was good at it, but not with a dragging foot, poor balance, clumsy hands and head pain so bad it could split an atom. So, for my own health and self care I stopped working ER last April.

I should mention here that the decisions I make not only impact me but also those who love me. I am lucky. I have a supportive family, friends and an amazing husband who loves me and goes through each of these storm days, doctor visits, hard decisions just like I do. In many ways I think it is harder on him as he wants so badly to make things easier for me.

This has changed the way my husband and I envision our future together. Who would have thought that we would be spending our time wondering if we should be living in a house designed for someone in a wheelchair or should we live somewhere with less snow so it will be easier to get around safely after surgery. I get it that nobody really knows the future but this tumor has made all of that uncertainty so real. Knowing that this thing exists is like having a third person in the marriage making decisions for us.

Having this tumor impacts my family, my friends, my work, my finances, my fun, my plans for the future, my everything. It is non-discriminatory in who it drags through the mud with it.

So back to the central question, at what point does it make sense to risk the surgery?

So far I have been saying that I will have the surgery when I have persistent motor function problems like weakness, paralysis or incontinence (yikes) and happily I don't have those. But lately I have been having so many sensory problems I have started to wonder if it makes more sense to focus my energy on healing from the surgery than to focus my energy on constantly managing the symptoms. In fact, since starting to work on this presentation a couple months ago my symptoms have definitely become more persistent. I am closer now to having the surgery than I ever have been and in my appointment tomorrow with Dr Rhines I will once again have to make the hardest decision of my life.

It's a strange thing to be the one deciding when it is right to have surgery. It's not like a broken leg or appendicitis where the decision is pretty clear. Unfortunately those of us with spinal cord tumors who are functioning well motor wise but pretty miserable sensory wise end up having to make a decision that feels like an educated roll of the dice.

Because as Dr Rhines has told me, "The surgery will not be a free lunch."

No one can tell me what my life will be like afterward.

Will I be paralyzed?
Will I die?
Will I be able to breathe on my own?
Or, will I walk out of surgery with basically the same
symptoms I have right now only knowing that I am tumor
free?

Gisela recently told me that symptoms caused by spinal
cord tumors are 'insidious'. I've been thinking about that a
lot. She's right. I have adapted over the years to the
symptoms and there is now a new normal (and that new
normal is very abnormal!). For example, I don't get on
ladders or even step stools anymore because if I turn my
head while on them I lose my sense of where I am in space
which is obviously not a good idea on a ladder. I don't ride
a bike or roller blade anymore for the same reason. I keep
a cane in my car in case my legs get weak on me when I
am out and about. I need a cane most days when walking
in the woods because the ground is not level making it
easy for me to catch my foot and stumble. I don't have a
day job anymore. And It's hard for me to make social
plans because I don't know how I'll be doing day by day
and it embarrasses me to cancel plans because I don't feel
good.

What is really fascinating to me and what makes my
decision about surgery so difficult is that on some days I'm
great. And on those days I am certain that there is no way
I will have the surgery. I mean look at me – I'm walking
without a cane, running on the treadmill, whatever. Then a
couple days later I need a cane to safely get around the
house.

All of this has challenged me to the core.

It's tempting to take some time here to give the "Hallmark Hall of Fame" version of this experience. You know the one where the young vibrant woman gets a tumor and something inspiring happens. I could do that because it is partly true. Having a life changing diagnosis can have that effect on people if you are vulnerable enough to let it.

For example - I've learned to accept help when offered. I've learned to say no to things that will drain me. I've learned to have hard conversations. I've learned to rest when I'm tired because fatigue makes everything worse. I've learned that I'm not responsible for how other people react to my diagnosis. I've learned that there is a difference between pain and suffering.

I prioritize how I want to spend my time while I am as able bodied as possible because I am constantly considering the fact that my current state of health is as good as it will ever be. I will never be more able bodied than I am at present so I better take advantage of it.

I believe that Health attracts health. I go to the gym. I meditate every day. I practice yoga every day. I have fun. I take vacations. Because the healthier I am – the healthier I am. I could go on and on with what this thing has taught me.

Walking away from ER nursing ended up being fine because my true passion in life is a form of weaving using knots instead of a loom. I work out anxiety related to the diagnosis in my knotting. I believe that I am attempting to regain some control over the uncontrollable nature of life by taking loose ends of cord and forming them into patterns. Since walking away from the day job my art work and business have done better than ever, which is great.

But if that is all that I talked about today I would not be telling you what it is really what it is like to live with a spinal cord tumor. I would be only telling you the Hollywood version. I'd like to read excerpts of email conversations I have had with two women who have tumors in the same place as mine and are also struggling with the decision about surgery.

We call ourselves the 3D Amigas because we have lots of things in common: Our names all start with D, we are all about the same age, we all have chosen not to have children and we all have a tumor in the same crappy spot. Or as the docs like to call it, "tumors in a high priced real estate area."

I had known about the tumor for four years before I found anyone else living with one. It was through the Spinal Cord Tumor Association's Online Forum that I met a woman from Boston and a woman from Sydney, Australia. I don't know what I would do without my 3D Amigas. We email regularly. We can talk about our situation with each other in a way that we can't with anyone else. My 2nd piece of advice to anyone with a spinal cord tumor is to connect with someone who is living through the same thing you are. It is less lonely.

Before I end by reading these conversations, I want to thank my 3D Amigas who have graciously and bravely given me permission to share their experience with you.

And I would like to thank MD Anderson for having this conference and for this opportunity to speak to you today from my heart.

The 3D Amigas Email Conversation:

From Me:

My symptoms flared last night and I'm having some trouble getting them under control today as well. It's so tiring. The head pain is overwhelming. Started last night and I just can't get a break from it. I'm trying meds, resting and staying distracted but it isn't helping. So I'm going to write to you and just let it all out and then hit the yoga mat.

I'm worrying a lot lately because when I turn my head to the right I get an electrical shock through my neck and arms. It's bad when I'm driving and I have to turn to look for oncoming traffic. I also am finding that if I flex my neck forward and to the right the left side of my chin and left cheek lose feeling. I also can't feel part of my left foot anymore. My left leg is killing me. And the shimmery electrical feelings in my legs never stop.

Jheesh, when I write it all out it seems like there is a reason for me to feel crappy! The fascinating part is that I was able to go to the gym and run yesterday So how can I function so well when I feel so bad?

Mostly, I'm worried that if I tell Dr Rhines all of this he will think it is time for the surgery. When I type that out I feel a bit panicky inside. The other part of me dreads hearing that it is not time for surgery and I have to put up with this longer. Then I realize I have to put up with this for the rest of my life and it just feels very overwhelming right now. There really is no good answer to our situation, is there?

From my Amiga in Australia:

After feeling quite elated about my MRI results last week that showed no growth, I fell into a slump of depression afterwards. I'm sure it's something that you can relate to; it's good news yes, but then it hit me again - I have a tumor. It may be benign, but the treatment is still the same - surgery. It's still as unpalatable as it was back in January when I was diagnosed.

I'm just back to living with it again, and managing it so that I can feel as normal as possible, which for me entails regular exercise, sleep and a healthy diet.

So that's where I am now - betwixt and between. I still wonder what the future holds for me, for all of us.

From my Amiga in Boston:

I can completely relate to the depression as the reality of our situations is indeed harsh, scary and unbelievably stressful. Not a day goes by that I don't think about my tumor, but, it's no longer in the forefront anymore, as it was for the first several months after my diagnosis.

My best suggestion is to treat yourself well, and to do whatever it takes at any given time to minimize the fear and anxiety associated with living with the "known unknown." We all know what our future holds for us (surgery, at some point, it appears), but the timing, the magnitude and the outcomes of our journeys are all, unfortunately, TBD; it is indeed like "living in limbo," which for me, is an extremely uncomfortable place.

Finally, from my Amiga in Australia:

Your words were a real comfort to me when I read them this morning. Particularly that the outcome is known - surgery. That's been a consistent message all round from everyone, from the time I was diagnosed. What's unknown is the outcome of the surgery. But then again, so are a lot of things about life. Some days I am so ready for surgery, "Bring it on" I say. The quicker I get it over and done with, the quicker I can get onto recovery and the rest of my life.

But of course it's not that easy. Like the both of you, in my heart of hearts, I cannot justify surgery at the moment. So, I just have to learn to live with it, befriend it further, whatever it takes!

OTHER RESOURCES

Collaborative Ependymoma Resource Network (CERN)
cern-foundation.org

Spinal Cord Tumor Association
The Spinal Cord Tumor Association Facebook page is a
closed group for people with tumors. I have found it to be
a supportive environment.
www.spinalcordtumor.org

ABOUT THE AUTHOR

Dawn Standera is a small business owner, a nurse, an artist, a wife, a daughter, a sister, and a proud mother of two rowdy dogs. While she never intended to be a writer, she acknowledges that sometimes in life, a calling chooses us.